Heroes and Villains of the

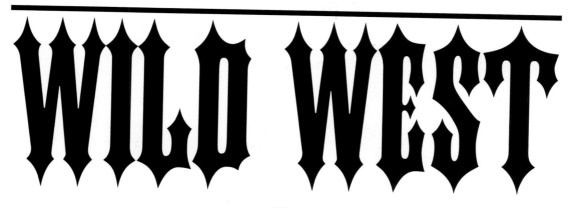

Wild Bill Hickok

by John Hamilton

ABDO & Daughters
PUBLISHING

Published by Abdo & Daughters, 4940 Viking Dr., Suite 622, Edina, MN 55435.

Copyright ©1996 by Abdo Consulting Group, Inc., Pentagon Tower, P.O. Box 36036, Minneapolis, Minnesota 55435. International copyrights reserved in all countries. No part of this book may be reproduced in any form without written permission from the publisher. Printed in the United States.

Cover Photo by: Archive Photos
Inside Photos by:
Bettmann: pp. 7, 13, 15, 19, 21, 23
Archive Photos: pp. 5, 11, 17, 28
John Hamilton: pp. 25, 27

Edited by Ken Berg

Library of Congress Cataloging–in–Publication Data
Hamilton, John, 1959–
  Wild Bill Hickok / John Hamilton
  p. cm. — (Heroes & villains of the wild West)
Includes bibliographical references (p. 31) and index.
ISBN: 1-56239-562-9
1. Hickok, Wild Bill. 1837–1876—Juvenile literature. 2. Peace officers—West (U.S.)—Biography—Juvenile literature.   I. Title. II. Series: Hamilton, John. Heroes & villains of the wild West.
F594.H62H36 1996
978'.02'092—dc20
[B]
                                                          95-36370
                                                             CIP
                                                              AC

Contents

Introduction

 On July 21, 1865, a man waited on the public square in Springfield, Missouri. He stood more than six feet tall, and had a tight, muscular body like a spring coiled for action. He wore a flat-brimmed hat atop fine auburn hair parted in the middle, shoulder length, the style of the era among frontiersmen. He sported a long mustache that drooped under a hawklike nose, giving him a predatory look. Slung around his waist was a scarlet silk sash, which supported a pair of ivory-handled .36-caliber Colt Navy revolvers. He wore his weapons butt-forward, always ready for a fast "twist" draw.

The man's name was James Butler Hickok, better known as Wild Bill, Prince of Pistoleers. He was a man of action who killed without hesitation or regret. He was a quick-draw dead shot who could put a straight row of holes in a target at 25 paces. But what really made Hickok "a bad man to fool with" was his cool attitude under fire. He had nerves of steel.

Pioneer of the Great Plains, Union scout and spy in the Civil War, lawman, express rider, showman. Wild Bill Hickok was all these and more. He seldom took unnecessary risks; he preferred sitting with his back to the wall, and he poured drinks with his left hand, leaving his right ready for action. When forced to act, he was ruthless, shooting first and asking questions later, if ever. When he drew his weapon, it was with one aim: to kill.

On that hot summer day in Springfield, Hickok stood ready for what would become a classic Western pistol duel. His adversary was a man by the name of Dave Tutt, an ex-Confederate soldier, gambler and ruffian, and also a crack shot with a pistol. The night before, Hickok had cleaned out Tutt in a game of poker.

James Butler "Wild Bill" Hickok.

The two men had argued over past debts, and at one point Tutt snatched Wild Bill's prized Waltham pocket watch. This slap at his honor made Hickok "shoot'n mad." He demanded his watch back. Tutt only laughed and walked away from the table. Hickok controlled his temper (just barely), not wanting to start a gunfight inside the saloon.

The next day, Hickok heard that Tutt was aiming to walk across the town square at noon, wearing the watch as a trophy. Rumor also had it that Tutt was out to kill Wild Bill by provoking him into a fight. If it was a fight Tutt wanted, he got it.

Hickok stood on the edge of the square, waiting, both guns in plain sight. Sure enough, at noon Tutt appeared, sporting Wild Bill's watch. Hickok warned him not to cross the square. Tutt ignored the threat and started walking forward. Suddenly, he went for his gun. Fast as lightning, Wild Bill drew his revolver and fired. Both shots went off at the same time, sounding as one. Tutt's missed.

Tutt fell dead in the dust, drilled through the heart. Wild Bill, sensing more danger, and without even waiting to see if his bullet had found its mark, whirled on his heels and pointed his gun at Tutt's friends before they could draw. "Aren't you satisfied, gentlemen?" shouted Bill, keeping his cool. "Put up your shootin-irons, or there'll be more dead men here." The men backed off, and Wild Bill walked away unharmed.

Hickok was arrested shortly afterwards, but a jury later found him not guilty of manslaughter. The verdict didn't sit well with some folks. They were appalled that a duel to the death could take place in their town. Some branded Hickok a low-down killer.

Wild Bill was sensitive to such criticism. Later he would write, "I suppose I am called a red-handed murderer, which I deny. That I have killed men I admit, but never unless in absolute self-defense, or in the performance of an official duty. I never, in all my life, took any mean advantage of an enemy."

Hickok tried to become town marshal of Springfield, perhaps to repair his reputation, but lost in the election. A few months later, he packed up his belongings and headed west, toward the rough-and-tumble cowtowns of Kansas.

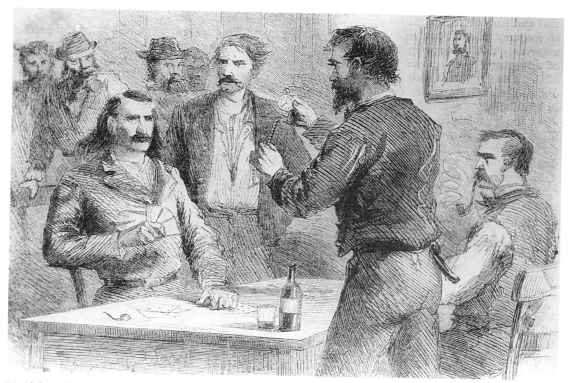

Wild Bill Hickok, seated with cards in his hand, watches as gambler Dave Tutt snatches Hickok's prized Waltham pocket watch after a poker match in Springfield, Missouri. The incident led to the famous shootout in the town square the next day.

Boyhood

James Butler Hickok was born to Polly and William Hickok on May 27, 1837 in the tiny farming town of Homer, Illinois. (Today it's called Troy Grove.) His father was a storekeeper, but the family moved to a farm shortly after James was born. James had three brothers and two sisters: Oliver, Horace, Lorenzo, Celinda, and Lydia.

When James reached age 10, he and his brothers lived in a log cabin close to the family farm. They went to school and also worked on neighboring farms for extra money.

Even when he was very young, James loved guns. With the money he earned, he bought his first pistol. Almost every day he ran off to the woods to practice his marksmanship. He used his skills to bring back fresh game for the family, including squirrels, rabbits, deer and prairie chickens. James enjoyed being alone among the trees. He began to find a deep confidence in himself, something that would be very important to him later in life.

After doing farm work during the day, James joined his father at night on the Underground Railroad, which was a group of people who helped escaping slaves. The Hickoks had a secret cellar in their house in which to hide the runaways. It was dangerous to assist slaves because armed bounty hunters were always on the prowl. The Hickoks once were fired at while moving some slaves in a wagon, but they escaped unharmed while the angry bounty hunters moved on to the next town, empty handed.

When James was 14, his older brother Oliver left for California to try to find his fortune in the gold rush. James took his place as a laborer on a neighbor's farm. Here something occurred that showed the young Hickok's character and spirit. His nephew wrote of the incident: "He and his brother had spent many hours swimming in the little river near their home. He was a fine swimmer. . . One day after a hard rain Jim and the boys of the neighborhood were swimming in the swollen stream. One of the young men from the party was from Peru, Illinois. He was a good swimmer, and amused himself by bullying the younger boys, and ducking them under the water. Wylie, the son of a Scotch immigrant, could not swim, but amused himself by wading and splashing in the shallower puddles. The Peru joker shoved him into deeper water, and Wylie promptly went under. The bully frightened, left the water, and started dressing. Uncle Jim jumped in and rescued Wylie, brought him safely to shore, and then walked over to Mr. Bully, picked him up clothes and all and threw him into the stream."

Out in the World

In 1852, James' father died. It was up to him and his brothers to operate the farm. Once he found work with a company that was constructing the Illinois and Michigan Canal. But James became angry because of the owner's cruelty to livestock and pushed him into the waterway. He returned to the farm, but by then, bored with small-town life, was eager to head west and find his own destiny.

James stuck with the farm until 1856. He and brother Lorenzo set off on foot to Kansas, anxious to buy land. Lorenzo eventually returned home to Illinois, but James remained, joining the Free State movement, which was trying to keep Kansas from becoming a state approving of slavery.

For a time, James again returned to farming and became a respectable citizen. He was even elected town constable of Monticello Township.

In 1858 Hickok gave up agriculture for good and moved to Leavenworth, Kansas. He found work as a teamster, driving wagons and stagecoaches over the Santa Fe and Oregon Trails for the firm of Russell, Majors and Waddell. It was while working this job that he met the great scout Kit Carson and future legend Buffalo Bill Cody. He and Cody became lifelong friends, as they had so much in common. They were both excellent scouts and crack shots, and shared many of the same experiences out on the open Plains. Cody soon went on to become a Pony Express rider, while Hickok remained a coach and freight driver.

Driving wagons was very dangerous out on the frontier. There was always the threat of bandits and hostile Indians. Once Hickok was attacked by a huge bear. He killed the beast with his knife, but was badly injured in the process. The company gave him light duties and sent him to Rock Creek Station in Nebraska Territory for recuperation.

Hickok as a scout, dressed in buckskins.

Fight at Rock Creek

In 1861, Hickok became involved in what would be known as the "McCanles Massacre." It was here, at the freight company's Rock Creek Station, that Hickok's legend truly began.

A shady character by the name of David McCanles sold a parcel of land to the Pony Express, but claimed to be having trouble collecting back payments from the newly formed express company. He decided to take the land back by force. He and two henchmen, each heavily armed with shotguns and pistols, arrived at Rock Creek Station and provoked a fight with Hickok.

History is fuzzy about what happened next. Most historians agree McCanles and his two cronies attacked Hickok simultaneously, guns blazing. But the young gunfighter kept his cool and put his fantastic marksmanship to good use. When the smoke cleared, Hickok was the only one left standing.

News of the shootout caused a sensation back East. Newspapers ran exaggerated stories of the McCanles Massacre. Some even had Wild Bill fighting off an entire gang of 10 desperadoes. At first Hickok wasn't too happy with all the attention he was getting. But his reputation as a crack shot and champion of law-and-order had begun.

In this greatly exaggerated woodcut by famed Civil War artist Alfred R. Waud, Wild Bill struggles for his life against the McCanles "gang."

"Wild Bill"

After the incident at Rock Creek, Hickok signed up for duty in the Civil War. He joined the Union Army as a sharpshooter, scout and teamster. He also worked as a spy, sneaking behind Confederate lines to discover enemy troop strength and positions. Because of his speed and accuracy with a pistol during the war, he soon became famous as the "fastest gun alive."

It was during his time in the Union Army that Hickok got the nickname "Wild Bill." In the spring of 1862, he was driving a wagon train full of Union supplies. In Jackson County, Missouri, the wagons were captured by Rebel forces. Hickok escaped and made his way to nearby Independence, Missouri, where he rounded up a band of well-armed volunteers. Together with this private army, Hickok recaptured the supply wagons from the Rebels the next morning.

While waiting around in Independence, Hickok spotted a crowd in front of a saloon. He was told that there had been a fight earlier and that the bartender had supported the losing side. Now the winning ruffians were out for the bartender's blood.

Hickok rushed into the saloon, drew his pistols, and demanded that the mob halt the lynching. A few foolish drunks moved forward anyway. Hickok fired his pistols into the ceiling, stopping them cold. He told the crowd to disperse or he would shoot the next man who moved forward. The mob, angry and grumbling, decided to call it a day. Hickok told the terrified bartender to come out (the barkeep had been hiding behind the bar). Hickok lectured the man on his poor choice of friends, then left.

Later that night, during a meeting of concerned citizens to discuss that afternoon's incident, a woman stood up and yelled, "Good for you, Wild Bill!" Never mind that Hickok's first name was James; the nickname stuck.

That's one story. Another one goes like this: Both James and his brother Lorenzo worked for the Union Army as wagon masters. To tell the difference, people began calling James "Wild Bill" and Lorenzo "Tame Bill." There are other stories as well, but what is known for a fact is that after the war, James Butler Hickok went by the name of Wild Bill.

Out of the army, Hickok made money gambling in Springfield, Missouri, until the celebrated duel with Dave Tutt. After his acquittal for the shooting, Wild Bill headed farther west.

Hickok soon found himself working for the U.S. Army at Fort Riley, Kansas. He was appointed deputy U.S. marshal, and also served as a scout for several military leaders, including General George Armstrong Custer.

Wild Bill was very well known by this time, thanks to his adventures. The newspapers also helped make him famous, printing all kinds of outrageous exaggerations. Everywhere he went he seemed to stand out. In

Wild Bill Hickok

a letter home, an officer at Fort Riley wrote: "By the way, I forgot to tell you about our guide—the most striking object in camp. Six feet, lithe, active, sinewy, daring rider, dead shot with pistol and rifle, long locks, fine features and mustache, buckskin leggins, red shirt, broad-brim hat, two pistols in belt, rifle in hand—he is a picture. He goes by the name of Wild Bill, and tells wonderful stories of his horsemanship, fighting and hair-breadth escapes. We do not, however, feel under any obligation to believe them all."

In fact, Wild Bill was a practical joker, and loved to tell tall tales. Whenever newspaper reporters asked him questions, Hickok delighted in pulling their legs. (He once told a gullible writer that he'd killed over 100 men. It was a ridiculous claim, showing Wild Bill's mischievous sense of humor.) Many of his stories found their way into print and, of course, the reading public ate it up. Wild Bill's reputation grew and grew, until he was practically a living legend.

Kansas Lawman

During the second half of the 1800's, there was a huge demand for beef in the cities back East and on the West Coast. To fill the need, Texas ranchers drove their herds of longhorn steers northward along the Chisholm Trail, which stretched from the Rio Grande River to Abilene, Kansas.

As rail lines were steadily built westward, cowtowns began springing up like weeds. These were places where the cattlemen could sell their herds and have them shipped off by train for the rest of the journey to the cities.

The cowtowns all looked pretty much alike. They had a single unpaved street running east and west along the railroad track. On hot summer days, the dust was sometimes ankle deep; when it rained the street turned into a muddy mess. Special places were built where the cattlemen and buyers could meet to do their business. Many dance halls and gambling saloons were on the north side of town, "on the wrong side of the tracks."

Hard-working cowboys drove the cattle herds along the Chisholm Trail. When they finally rode into town, they got paid. After so many weeks out on the open range, the cowpokes felt a need to let off steam. The saloons of the cowtowns satisfied this need. Unfortunately, there was a lot of violence because of all the hard drinking and gambling.

In 1871 Wild Bill became marshal of Abilene, Kansas, the best-known cowtown of them all. Two years earlier he served as a lawman in Hays City, Kansas, helping rid the place of rowdy Texas cowboys. Abilene, though, would be one tough town to tame. Ruffians were constantly riding down main street, whooping and hollering and shooting their guns in the air. Crime was everywhere. (The previous marshal was found one day with his head cut off.) In rode Wild Bill, determined to make the cowboys behave.

Hickok during his days in Cheyenne, Wyoming.

Hickok ruled with an iron fist. He showed a lot of courage and used his skill as a marksman to protect the citizens of Abilene. He strictly enforced the laws, especially the one banning the carrying of guns inside the city limits. He tried to keep the gamblers honest, and he ran vagrants and troublemakers out of town—sometimes at gunpoint.

Wild Bill made a lot of enemies in Abilene. He knew he had to be careful to protect himself. He always walked down the middle of the street, staying away from the sidewalk where a killer might leap out of a dark alley.

On the night of October 5, 1871, Wild Bill broke up a disturbance caused by several unruly Texans. Their leader, Phil Coe, had been firing his pistol into the air. Hickok demanded that Coe give up his firearm. Coe refused and went out into the street, surrounded by a howling mob of Texans.

Wild Bill faced off against his foe. Coe raised his gun to fire, but Marshal Hickok was too quick. Instantly his pair of revolvers were out and blazing. Coe fell to the ground, mortally wounded. The Texan got off one shot, but it passed harmlessly through Hickok's coat. Suddenly, Wild Bill saw a shadowy figure dart from a dark alley. Hickok turned and fired. Sadly, he had killed his own deputy by mistake. Hickok whirled on the drunken mob, leveled his twin six shooters at them. He shouted, "If any of you want the balance of these pills, come and get them!" The crowd quickly broke up.

Raging with anger at the killing of his deputy, Hickok went wild. He swept through the saloons and gambling houses, shutting them down and kicking everybody out. Few argued with him; those that did he knocked to the ground. Others just ran away. This time, the *real* Wild Bill lived up to the legend.

In time, the residents of Abilene grew tired of the rowdy Texans *and* Wild Bill. In 1872 they passed a law banning the cattle drives through their town. Since the Texans were no longer a threat, Abilene didn't need the services of a "high-priced" marshal anymore. Wild Bill Hickok was out of a job.

Showman

The West was changing. By the mid-1870's things were quickly becoming more civilized. The quick-draw gunslinging skills of men like Wild Bill Hickok weren't really needed anymore.

By now Wild Bill was very famous, but in those days one couldn't live on fame alone. He knew he had to find work. Starting in 1872, Hickok toured with several shows around the eastern United States. In 1873 he starred on the stage with Buffalo Bill Cody and Texas Jack Omohundro in "The Scouts of the Plains."

But Wild Bill soon grew weary of show business. He'd lived his life on the wide-open Plains, and in his heart he knew that's where he belonged. In 1874 Hickok left the stage to venture out West once more.

Left to right: Elisha Green, Wild Bill Hickok, Buffalo Bill Cody, Texas Jack Omohundro, and Eugene Overton.

Gold Rush

On March 5, 1876, Wild Bill, at age 38, married Agnes Lake Thatcher in Cheyenne, Wyoming. Hickok had many lady friends during his years on the Plains, but it was Agnes, five years older than he, who finally corralled him. The widow of a circus owner, Agnes rode horses and performed acrobatics. The two first met in Abilene, Kansas, and then in Rochester, New York, while Hickok was working in Buffalo Bill's stage show. They crossed paths again years later in Cheyenne, where they decided to marry. There were those who couldn't believe Wild Bill Hickok could ever settle for marriage. In fact, the minister who officiated at the ceremony wrote in the Methodist church register, "I don't think they meant it."

But by this time Hickok was beginning to feel his age. His eyesight was failing, and he knew he couldn't make a living forever on his reputation as a gunfighter. If he was ever to sink roots into a calmer domestic environment, he had to find some way to make a lot of money, and quickly.

After a brief honeymoon in Cincinnati, Ohio, Wild Bill left Agnes to head west one more time, to the Black Hills of the Dakota Territories. He hoped to strike it rich prospecting gold so he could return to his wife and retire.

Two years earlier, in 1874, General George Custer led an expedition into the Black Hills, which sit on the western edge of what is today South Dakota. In violation of a treaty with the Sioux Indians, Custer entered their sacred land on a survey mission, and while there discovered gold. The news spread like wildfire, and before long prospectors by the thousands were pouring into the area.

At first, the army tried keeping the gold diggers out, but after only a few months there were too many arrivals. The Sioux, rightfully angry, began attacking the invaders. The military was forced to protect the white settlers, those who didn't have a right to be there in the first place.

The gold rush town of Deadwood, Dakota Territories, 1876.

Mining camps sprang up all over the Black Hills. Some grew into towns. Of these, Deadwood was one of the most important. With steep, thickly forested hills rising up and surrounding it, the town is situated at the end of a narrow gulch, nestled up against a canyon wall.

In less than a year, Deadwood was a gold rush mecca, and business was booming. Main Street was a bare dirt wagon path. People swarmed like ants, dodging the ox carts, carriages, wagons and horses jamming the street. For every store there were three saloons, all filled with prospectors eager to spend their new-found riches. Like the early cowtowns of Kansas, Deadwood was almost completely lawless. Fistfights were always erupting in public, and everyone packed a gun for self-defense. People died of "lead poisoning" nearly every week.

It was into this scene that Wild Bill appeared in July of 1876. He tried panning gold, but wasn't too successful. Mostly he spent his time in the saloons and gambling houses. Some historians say Hickok was hanging around, waiting to see if Deadwood would appoint him town marshal, a job for which he was much more qualified than panning gold.

Popular legend has it that while in Deadwood, Wild Bill had a love affair with the noted frontierswoman Calamity Jane. Some say they even had a child together. That the two met there is no doubt. However, most historians say their relationship was strictly on friendly terms. Hickok loved his new bride, Agnes, dearly, and there is no proof that he ever wandered from his devotion to her.

A miner panning for gold in a stream. Wild Bill tried his luck panning for gold in Deadwood, but never struck it rich.

Dead Man's Hand

On August 2, Wild Bill sauntered into Deadwood's No. 10 Saloon, looking for a game of poker. A table of men allowed him to join in, but refused to give up any of their seats. Hickok was forced to sit with his back to the door, something he almost never did. He'd already told people he believed his life was in danger in Deadwood. "Those fellows over across the creek have laid it out to kill me," he said, "and they're going to do it or they ain't. Anyway, I don't stir out of here unless I'm carried out." Despite his fears, Hickok took a chair and began playing.

Soon a man by the name of Jack McCall strode into the tavern. Some said he had a personal grudge with Hickok. Others claim that shady people in Deadwood paid McCall to do away with the famous lawman. Perhaps they were afraid that if he became marshal, Hickok would clean up the town and make it tougher on the lawless.

Whatever the reason, McCall crept up behind Wild Bill and put a pistol to the back of his head. "Take that!" he shouted, pulling the trigger. The great Hickok was killed instantly, his body slumping forward and spilling his hand of cards face-up on the table. The bullet passed through Hickok's brain and lodged in the wrist of another poker player, William Massey, who never had it removed because of the notoriety.

The cards in Wild Bill's final hand of poker are known today as the "Dead Man's Hand." Local legend has always said that the cards included black aces over black eights. However, the actual cards he held are not known. The Adams Museum in Deadwood has a set of cards on display that were donated by a man who supposedly went into the saloon and collected them shortly after the shooting. Those cards are the ace of clubs, ace of diamonds, eight of spades, eight of hearts, and queen of hearts. But as the curator of the Adams Museum puts it, "Only Wild Bill knows for sure what was in the 'Dead Man's Hand,' and he's not talking."

Wild Bill's final resting place in Mount Moriah Cemetery, overlooking Deadwood, South Dakota.

Jack McCall was captured and put on trial by a miner's court, as there were no judges or law of any kind in Deadwood at that time. Amazingly, McCall was found innocent. During the trial he claimed that Hickok had killed his brother and had threatened to kill him as well. McCall said he shot Hickok in self-defense.

The verdict didn't sit well with law-abiding residents in Deadwood. Rumors spread that the jury had been bribed by the same people that had paid McCall to shoot Wild Bill. But before they could do anything about it, McCall had fled, fearing that he would be strung up by a lynch mob.

Later, McCall was arrested again in Laramie, Wyoming. Because Deadwood was an outlaw town, the miner's court trial had been declared illegal. The citizens had no legal right to be there since the Black Hills were still technically Sioux land. McCall was tried once more in a legal courtroom in Yankton, Dakota Territories. Found guilty this time, he was hanged March 1, 1877.

Today Wild Bill Hickok is buried atop Mount Moriah Cemetery overlooking Deadwood. His good friend, Colorado Charley Utter, paid for the funeral and had a wooden headboard placed on Hickok's grave. It reads: "Wild Bill-J.B. Hickock (*sic*). Killed by the assassin Jack McCall in Deadwood Black Hills. August 2nd 1876. Pard we will meet again in the Happy Hunting ground to part no more. Good Bye—Colorado Charlie. C.H. Utter."

Stories about James Butler Hickok have been told and retold for over 100 years. Today we relive his adventures mostly in movies and television. Some stories are true, some are not. What we know for sure is that he was a scout, a lawman, a showman. Call him a hero or a killer, he was Wild Bill Hickok, truly the Prince of Pistoleers.

The Wild Bill Hickok Memorial Statue in Deadwood, South Dakota.

The Wild West of
Wild Bill Hickok

Illinois
Homer (Troy Grove)
Iowa
Missouri
Independence
Kansas City
Springfield
Leavenworth
Rock Creek Station
Fort Riley
Abilene
Monticello
Chisholm Trail
South Dakota
Deadwood
Nebraska
North Platte
Hays City
Kansas
Denver
Colorado
Wyoming
Cheyenne

Glossary

bounty hunter

Someone who hunts criminals or outlaws for money. Before and during the Civil War, escaped slaves were considered criminals in the Southern states and were chased by bounty hunters.

Civil War

The war fought in the United States between Union forces (the North) and the Confederacy (the South), between 1861 and 1865. The dispute over whether or not people should own slaves was a major cause of the war.

Colt Navy revolver

A very popular pistol in the Old West, manufactured by Samuel Colt. Lighter and easier to handle than other pistols of the time, the Colt Navy was a .36-caliber six-shot weapon with a 7.5" barrel. It was called the Navy revolver most likely because a large shipment was ordered and used by the United States Navy. Wild Bill Hickok liked these guns because they were easy to handle and had hard-hitting accuracy.

Free State movement

Before the Civil War, a Free State was one that didn't allow slaves. Before they became states, many territories, especially Kansas, saw a lot of violence between groups that argued over slavery.

frontiersman

A person who lived alone out on the open frontier. Many served as scouts and guides for settlers or military forces heading west. Some famous frontiersmen included Wild Bill Hickok, Kit Carson, and Buffalo Bill Cody.

Great Plains

A large, mostly flat area in central North America, reaching from the Central Plains just west of the Mississippi to the eastern edge of the Rocky Mountains.

manslaughter

The unlawful killing of another person without the intent to do so beforehand.

pistoleer

A gunfighter, usually a quick-draw artist who could shoot with great accuracy.

Pony Express

A system of mail delivery that used several relay stations where riders could change to a fresh horse and not have to rest.

twist draw

Used when pistols were worn with the butt end pointing forward. The gunfighter drew the opposite arm across his body and grabbed the pistol, then "twisted" it out of the holster, moving it up and forward to point at the enemy. In skilled hands, this was a very quick way of drawing weapons.

Bibliography

Baker, Anne Marie, Curator. Adams Museum, Deadwood, South Dakota.

Conlan, Roberta, Editor. *The Wild West.* New York: Time-Life Books, 1993.

Encyclopaedia Britannica, Volume V, p. 28.

Fielder, Mildred. *Wild Bill Hickok.* Centennial Distributors, Deadwood, South Dakota, 1974.

Flanagan, Mike. *Out West.* New York: Harry N. Abrams, Inc, 1987.

Hickok, Howard L., *The Hickok Legend.* Unpublished manuscript in the possession of his son, Major James Butler Hickok, U.S.M.C.

Lee, Robert. *Gold, Gals, Guns, Guts.* Deadwood, South Dakota: Deadwood-Lead '76 Centennial, Inc, 1984.

Parker, Watson. *Deadwood: The Golden Years.* University of Nebraska Press: Lincoln and London, 1981.

Rosa, Joseph G. *Age of the Gunfighter.* New York: Smithmark Publishers, Inc., 1993.

Rosa, Joseph G. *The Gunfighter: Man or Myth?* University of Oklahoma Press: Norman and London, 1969.

Rosa, Joseph G. *They Called Him Wild Bill.* University of Oklahoma Press: Norman and London, 1974.

Wheeler, Keith. *The Scouts.* New York: Time-Life Books, 1978.

Index